THE 2023
ONE PAGE POETRY
Anthology

ONE PAGE POETRY

EDITED BY COLIN GRAHAM

One Page Poetry/The 2023 One Page Poetry Anthology
www.onepagepoetry.com
Printed in the United States of America

The 2023 One Page Poetry Anthology/ One Page Poetry -- 1st ed.

ISBN 9798869897572 Print Edition

All proceeds from the sale of this book will go to the World Wildlife Fund and Oceana, two organizations dedicated to the protection of endangered species and the preservation of their natural habitats.

In celebration of the beautiful art of poetry

Publisher's Note

Out of respect for the amazing poets who have contributed to this anthology, the individual poems have not been edited in any way and fully represent the original presentation of each poet. In some cases, poems required formatting to fit the size restrictions of the book and the ebook, but in no way did this formatting change the original wording or grammatical presentation. Since the individual poets represented in this anthology continue to own the copyright to their poems, the poems are not exclusive to this publication, and we encourage the poets to distribute their work as widely as they choose.

A Special Thanks to Our 2023 Judges:

monique jonath is a twenty-one-year-old queer black poet from Oakland, CA who is currently a senior studying gender and sexuality studies and psychology at Brown University. They started writing poetry as a joke in early high school, but it quickly developed into one of their biggest passions. They were a finalist for the position of Oakland Youth Poet Laureate in both 2018 and 2019. They were also a finalist and a winner of the writer-voted Sixfold poetry contest. In their free time, they are a peer sexual health educator, contemporary and African dancer, and music enthusiast.

Mark Graham is a critically acclaimed novelist and poet who has been writing professionally since 1988. He has written and published five critically acclaimed novels: *The Harbinger* (Henry Holt & Co.), The *Missing Sixth* (Harcourt, Brace, & Jovanovich), *The Fire Theft* (Viking Penguin), *The Natanz Directive* (St. Martin's Press), and *The Five Portals* (Castle Knight Press). He has also written two acclaimed collections of poetry, *Parents Are Diamonds – Children Are Pearls.* (Amur Books) and *And Wrap Your Arms Around Living* (Castle Knight Press).

Ann Tinkham is a published author, ghostwriter, and editor based in Boulder, Colorado. Her fiction and essays have appeared in Apt, Denver Syntax, Edifice Wrecked, Foliate Oak, Lily Literary Review, Short Story Library, Slow Trains, Synchronized Chaos, The Adirondack Review, The Battered Suitcase, The Citron Review, The Literary Review, Toasted Cheese, Wild Violet, Word Riot, and others. Ann's essay, "The Tree of Hearts" was nominated for a Pushcart Prize and her story, "Afraid of the Rain" was nominated for Sundress's Best of the Net Anthology. She's the author of *Climbing Mountains in Stilettos* and two story collections, *The Era of Lanterns and Bells* and *Stories I Can't Show My Mother*.

This is Not America
Raya Yarbrough, Los Angeles, CA

This is not America,
this is twisted wood in sand.
This is 10 million years
in this stone, in my hand.
This is the dirt beneath the factory.
Dirt beneath the church.
Dirt which holds, refractory
to governmental girth.
We drive and we stride
and we fall and we ride
without thought,
on the crumbled blood of mountains.

But this is not America,
these are fathoms and tides.
These are homes of loons and otters
only human hands divide.
This is the hiss of reeds
a sea above a sea,
an old spiritual, moaning,
in the language of the Hickory.
From ancient river spines
boils brine from the fault,
and we have forgotten ourselves,
as the children of salt.

But this is not America,
this is 5:09pm
and the cobweb in the window
has caught fire again
in the lift of summer's nothings,
spectral breaths which lift the weave
to breathe through phantom tendons
on the edge of this eve.

Now the wind chimes, now a shadow
following the ring,
none of these have ever been at war
with anything.
I call to this land
by the name given to it
by the Bear and the Orca,
by the fox and the crow.
The name we can hold in our hands
in the driftwood
but we can never know.

Sahara
Cassie Lipton, Charlottesville, VA

One day, my body
will not remember it's anger
the way the Sahara
does not remember
it was once ocean.

One day, the seasickness
will become less violent,
the waves less treacherous,
as drop by drop you drain
from the space I've left open.

One day, I will step out
and the water will be ankle-deep.
Your memory is sea salt
on my face and in my hair
but drawing is no danger

One day, I will lay on the damp
sand, soft and pliable
and build castles of everything
I have become without you,
when I've washed away my anger.

And in a thousand years,
I will lie on the dunes
and feel the dry heat on my back
and it will be
as if you were
nothing.

Elemental

Jenna Martinez, Cleveland, Ohio

Aire

at eighteen, my mother runs away

to the border to marry my father.

the air that carries her to Laredo

seeps into the seeds of me.

I bloom into a small tornado.

breezes ferry me into soft beds and soft bodies.

in Mexico, a woman holds my palm

eres inquieta, she says.

I turn 33 in Death Valley.

the wind strikes the sand

into wisps the shape of snakes.

Fuego

the heat of Brooklyn

evaporates up the summer concrete

holding the steps of all of us

tumbling through the city.

I have a husband, a girlfriend, and a lover.

I am a giant.

I press my heavy foot onto the street

stepping over the bridges

that touch borough to borough.

unfurled, I expand across the city,

come to its borders and spill.

Agua

on the southside of San Antonio,

the curandera spins a bath for sweetness.

the petals fall onto the shower floor.

I toe the constellations at my feet.

bathed in honey,

I loosen the laces, untie myself

from my life, my marriage,

my pebble of earth.

I slip into dark waters.

Tierra

Rock, Paper, Scissors
Mridvi Khetan, Chicago, IL

Sometimes it's all a child's play
Rock
Paper
Scissors
Play it as you may

Her index and middle fingers casually separate to create a fissure,
a lens to see the landscape hidden below her flesh
The scissor-like fingers a part of the overpowering body

A body is nothing but a rock on this earth
Defeating every thing, every finger, every scissor

Until
the paper comes
A paper, the renewed life of nature
with the several inscriptions of men
has the fuel to render every rock useless
Because a body cowers behind papers
The red tape is the dictator
What am I, if not for a paper telling me I'm a citizen?
What am I, if not for a paper to show I'm educated?
What am I, if not for a paper to flaunt for my status?
A body is nothing without its papers
A rock is always defeated by paper

The mountains can vouch for it too
Those hefty structures always losing the game to the clouds
The mountains - a body - perpetually a rock
The clouds - a shapeshifter - mostly a paper enshrouding the peaks
There you have it, the rock defeated again

There is only one way to defeat the paper -
to stretch apart those fingers
Only when the scissors detach from the rock,
the fingers depart from the body
Can the scissors defeat the paper
Only when the talent detaches from the being,
when the art departs from the artist, from the red-taped helpless humans
Can it actually cut through the suffocating boundaries of the paper

So what's your move?
Rock, Paper or Scissors?

Paper Cuts
Maria Oglesby, Chapel Hill, NC

Depression hits everyone different

For some, it's a gut punch

I have a friend who is shattered by it. Every year when ice coats the ground and the heater goes tck tck tck she lies fragile as frost, unable to get out of bed without breaking.

For me, it's a paper cut.

You can go to work with a paper cut.

Sometimes, when you hold it closed, you can't even remember you have one.

You don't need to see a doctor for a paper cut

You can wrap it up

And usually, that helps.

But sometimes, there are too many to wrap.

When life sours, the lemon-juice sting of anxiety opens all the old ones up with a pang I can't ignore.

I wonder sometimes

Would you have to see a doctor if you had a thousand paper cuts?

What about 50?

What about five?

A cut for each friend left behind (a drop in a well I float above

A cut for the frantic background buzz of desperation

A cut for failure, each road in life a detour over a path uncrossed

A cut for the guilt that gnaws at my gut for each time my hungry temper bites

A cut for the children I might never be able to have

Where do you draw the line?

When does a paper cut become a wound

After 9/11
Joan Roger, Bainbridge, WA

"Tomorrow, and tomorrow, and tomorrow…" William Shakespeare

The digging went on for weeks, for months.
Tomorrow came and we grieved and raged
through that long winter. Our bodies became hungry,
so we ate toast and drank coffee; we showered
and washed our hair; we put on clean shirts,
slacks, shoes; we bought groceries, we slept,
we went to work, cold, tired, unmoored.
Wounds stopped weeping and scars formed.
And every day, babies were born. Children
went to school and played in the snow.
Mail was delivered and bills paid.
A day came when laugher was heard again,
and music. Lovers embraced in the night.
And even now, over twenty years later,
I don't understand what any of it signifies—
the something of this day
turning to the next—
but when I think of the firefighters
who climbed those burning buildings,
when I remember the people who opened their doors
to shelter strangers and the rescuers who risked their lives
sifting through the smoking debris,
then I know that despite the slow stride
of the body, despite the darkness, the grave,
despite all that threatens and pulls us apart,
there's something decent within us
that lives.

The World Could Be Beautiful
Dylan Lyons, New York, NY

The world could be beautiful,
but we let greed reign.
The rich rig the system
for their own gain.
Kids without food,
families without homes.
The growing debt smothers,
but we're all on our own.

The world could be beautiful,
but we let guns rule.
The fear lurks around us,
on the streets and at school.
Parents lose children,
children lose friends.
Is that the price of "freedom,"
these violent ends?

The world could be beautiful,
but we let hate thrive.
Anyone who's different
must fight to survive.
Racism runs deep,
down to the soil,
but the structures of power
feed off the turmoil.

The world could be beautiful,
but we're letting it burn.
Nature's decaying
as the earth turns.
We live for consumption,
for oil and gas,
so the storms just grow stronger
and take longer to pass.

The world could be beautiful,
if we switch up the play.
We could rewrite the rules
and demand a new day.
Replace hate with compassion
and swap greed for giving.
In a world this beautiful,
we'd truly be living.

Please Don't Touch
John Okhiulu, Oakland, CA

I'm fly!   Just look at me!
One modern molecular mess, Take a look!
I've found myself so you can see me all you want!
See my eyeliner pop!   See the way my locs dance!
Look if you want
but please don't touch.
Your hands might wipe me away
and derail the meticulous detail
I've fashioned for myself right here
in this skin.

Look, don't touch
As I carry my burning cross,
Heavy on once weightless shoulders
Watch as I carry it back to my burning house.
I tried your home on and it just didn't fit.

Wading through the storm of men,
Strangers they became, they
   pulled my shoulders close to them,
     might have even looked romantic as they
      ruffled my hair like one might do
      a child. They laughed.

I wanted to cry as you stood over me
My face pressed into the warm of your belly
Your hands held me together, you
Held my pieces as we walked
And I loved you more and more
You bade me safe
      Pleaded me worthy
      Fashioned me whole again.
And we danced as we spilled over one another
And we laughed as my cup runneth over
my goodness, what a night.

The fire
Cassi Clark, Breckenridge, CO

is a rite to womanhood
the fuel of grief
that keeps us moving
that keeps us participating.
What happens when the anger
fades away?
When we have so few fucks
to give we can't even say
we have no fucks.
When the fire has burned all
all the layers that give
in to your chiseling
words, social (con)forms.
What happens when the rage
 - the last bind
is gone with your influence.
What life will I live
when all my power is mine
and yours has no over?
The noisy peace
of full strong breath
birds, squirrels, wind in trees.
The sounds I choose.
The words I choose.
The life I choose.
A new social order

Left Field
Susan Drenna Gabriel Bunn, Annapolis, MD

Do not be afraid of the space you've been given.

The place
You find yourself in.
This.
Born of emptiness.

The time you were left heart bleeding.
History lives.
History breathes.
The moment of your death.
History is here.
Now.
In me.
The life that was stolen and all robbed since then.
These are the wounds of the world's unknowing.

Do not be afraid of the space you've been given.
The field you've been delivered to.
Here and now is all
Being.
Grounded in a sea of light attended
Spirit.
Busy paving your life in
Love.

AND
Harvey Nelson, Akron, OH

As a kid, I loved peanut butter on white bread,
Sticking to the roof of my mouth.
Strawberry jelly, on light brown toast,
Sweet and thick, licking it, as it dripped down my chin.

But peanut butter AND jelly.
Damn, that was a combination!

And that was only the beginning.
Eggs AND cream cheese on a bagel.
Mustard AND ketchup on a burger.
Pepperoni AND sausage on a pizza.

Lately, I've been trying out some other concoctions.

I sunk my teeth into,
Black lives matter AND support the police.
Capitalism AND social responsibility.
Pull yourself up AND we need to help each other.
Climate change is real AND the climate always changes.

Most recently I've dined on,
I want to hear you out AND I want to rip your head off.

There will always be rich AND there will always be poor.
At least relatively.
We are not a homogenized glass of milk.

So,
If you love your peanut butter.
Or,
If you love your jelly.

Take a chance,
Try a bite of AND.

Heart

Kate Proctor, London, England

Disease crept in,
And first hid small,
In dark warm corners,
Of lesser organs.
Waiting to spread charred and twisted fingers,
Around the body that gave us life.
But the heart stays strong,
And charges on.
A thousand silver layers,
From generous moons.
A wall galvanised with love and sorrow,
Wisdom and toil.
She is travelling somewhere,
Her heart like a train,
Through cities and fields,
Never slowing for platforms,
It does not yield,
To pleasures taken,
From quiet stations.
With hanging baskets,
That quiver in the wake,
Of the thundering engine.
Four chambers hammering,
Towards infinity.
No promise of gentle adventure,
We cannot help her,
But to wet her lips,

With thirsty sips,
She rattles alone.
Death appears but the heart battles on,
It does not slow,
But hastens to hammer against ribs,
Demanding more coal,
To keep the fire burning.
But the stoker tires,
And at last with a sigh,
The end of the line.
A platinum layer,
Around hearts left behind.

Look Up
Sarah Talbert, Jensen Beach, FL

Fall of heaven and earth

Your beauty wasn't tainted

It was hidden

We search, we grasp, we create

Only to make you look like us

We yell and fight

For freedoms that end up binding our hands

We're playing in the mud beneath our toes hoping to create castles and
kingdoms to fit our molds.

Our fingers caked in the dirt of our own mess

Like a child, face downcast,

We wait for a punishing blow of words,

"Clean yourself up."

But then,

You look down and you see.

Not in disgust or apathy

You look down then reach down.

You hold our faces in your hands and whisper,

"I see you.

Stop playing in places I didn't make for you.

Look up.

Stop chasing what you've made me to be.

Look up.

Stop squeezing me into something I'm not.

Look up.

I am good.

Everything that is good. I did that.

I am peace.

I do not withhold it but gladly give it.

I am creator.

And although it may look like I'm not in control,

You can see me if you release your tight grip on the castles you're building,

I've made better.

You're already loved

Already healed.

Already seen.

Look up."

Lamentation for the Immortal Wild Horses
Red Hawk, Monticello, AR

The Moon fades on the downslope
of his eye, like history
erasing a species from the fauna map.
Untroubled by bridle, stirrup, halter or barn,
by human stink or strain of plow or
curse of domestic ease,
he lengthens into full gallop, headed
across the rocky plateau, over
sawgrass and spindle flower,
down slope and wind,
a dawnhorse trailing a dewy field.
The wind is in his mane, dawn breaks
over his mortal flesh, steep slope

of muscle along flank, forearm and fetlock,
pure wide-nostril joy,
mute muscular motion,
surge of muscle, gristle and bone
through space and time into
an infinity of grace in the bloodline,
immortality in the beating beast-heart,
the unfailing and unending snort and
trot and gallop beneath the unchanging
Sun and Moon of desire and death, down
to the river water where the mares wait and

the colts huffle and snort, slurp water and
then rise up like clouds of nostril steam,
race up from the river to greet him
and gambol and play in the dawning light,

never suspecting they will die,
that they all are just passers-by
and the end of the wild Mustang draws nigh;
he nickers in a cloud of steaming breath
and they race with him, leaving death
waiting patiently with infinite trust,
knowing even iron soon turns to rust
and powerful bone to dust.

Paalam
Gabriella Guidero, Bellevue, WA

Waves, bows, palms pressed down
Sad tilts among heavy shoulders
Sunsets and cold hands.
The weight of love is unyielding, ruthless.
Watch an icicle snap against the frosty air of a warm cabin
Paalam. Water does not forgive the sorrow of connection.

Take Small Steps
Aisha Claire Robins, San Antonio, TX

Take small steps, for the doing,
not the going, and trust the
hesitation, knowing a helping hand
is there to keep you upright.

Take small steps, break it down,
keep it simple, and watch as
every action brings energy
that takes you away from stuck.

Take small steps, hard at first,
easier with each one, and
confidence grows by looking back
to where you started.

Take small steps, each one teaching,
each one testing resolve, and know
the direction can change, at any point
without a "Mother, may I?"

Now,
take small steps.

Remember Me
Elizabeth Goehner, Blaxland, Australia

I once was awed majestically, my Gift a treasured memory
I sheltered creatures all around and nurtured teeming life abound
I played and shimmered in the breeze and brushed the sky with fingered ease
With palette amber, red green and gold,
sweet blooms abundant in hues untold
I lent my trunk to lover's trust, a silent witness to their lust
Their whispered secrets safe I kept, dream guardian steadfast as they slept
But with morn break on warbled wing as kookaburras
augh and magpie sing
The wind brings news of hearts soon torn, the Sun now frowns and grey
clouds warn
For eyes have turned to greed and wealth and not in keeping with my health
They come with gnashing chainsaws bound, cruel vengeance strong to cut
me down
I quake and brace against the blade,
but crash to Earth where my feet were made
And reduced to pile through savage jaws, I am left to rot as my anguish roars
Then bores grind deep, to take my Soul,
skies gently weep as grief takes hold
While here I gave you air to breathe, but gone I leave your Lungs to heave!
My Mother yawns through hellish throat and gleans my scattered telling notes
That if Mankind take Us away, it too will be, their Dying Day.

This poem is about you
Tierney Caden, Epping, Australia

When I hear your voice on the phone now,
I remember those days when you were everything to me...
When I turned my life upside down for you,
Gave up my family, my friends, my career,
To make a new life with you so very far away.

I remember the day you left –
Tears pouring down my face,
Trying to comfort our crying children,
Wondering how it had come down to this.

I remember those lonely nights without you,
When depression settled over me like a shroud,
And I struggled to make it through every single day.

I remember finally finding the strength and resilience within myself
To carry on regardless, and to grow in confidence,
Which you had whittled away so easily without any care or thought.

And now when I hear your voice,
I feel very little – not love, not hate, not friendship, not enmity.

And that is the saddest thing of all.

Hopscotch

Jude Luttrell Bradley, Long Beach, CA

On wrong side of railroad tracks
separating chancy city from safe-ish suburbs,
two peppy eight-year-olds skip into shadow
cast by skyscraper housing projects,
on their way to raid candy dish in Auntie's flat.
Stooping to eye a pair of deflated pink rubber balls,
Spalding high bouncers, their high-flying hopes
are quickly punctured by experienced understanding . . .
balls too flattened for fun from everyday smashing
into improvised handball court: corrugated loading dock door.
Gamboling sisters turn metaphysical corner to Auntie's,
then scamper toward gang graffitied steel doorway,
spray-paint cyphers claiming territory for the damned.
Silvery entrance flanked habitually by dual gargoyle junkies.
One is in a full nod, his drooling mouth agape; the other mutters a curse.
Crossing the building's threshold,
schoolgirls collide with big bear man
bathed in panic cologne.
He bounces from the building,
trailed by wild-eyed woman in worn-out bathrobe.

Her squashed breast exposed, she tracks him;

one pale pink sponge curler dangles from snarled hair to forehead.

Her man prey bellows something the girls understand

only after he collapses at their feet in muddy red puddle:

She got a gun! Sweetie got a gun!

Accustomed to their ferocious neighborhood,

The girls make a game of trauma,

Missing only a beat or two,

they skedaddle to nab Auntie's candy,

hopscotching through hazards of life in the city.

Saving the Jellies
J Catherine Tetrault, Millis, MA

Spring tides carry the jellies
floating adrift upon white horses
Blue, pink, purple, clear
bells adorned with petals and sun rays
Swaying in skirts of seafoam
graceful arms move to rhythmic swells

Carefree, careless
seductive sea pulls them in
careening with the current
Flung onto sand and rocks
lingering as the tide recedes
forsaken like a lover's farewell kiss

Stranded
Vulnerable
Exposed
Hapless, helpless
silently shriveling
Sea Nettles still stinging

Who can save them?

Praying to the sea,
reclaim your lost ones and forgive their frailty
Praying to the sky,
ease their suffering and send rain

Praying to the universe,
spare their short lives for one more night of moonlit magic
Motionless jellies
emptied of life
taken too soon

There was no saving them.

Honoring their grace
by recalling the story
of their dance

They live on.

We Grow Back
Lucy Christopher, Sydney, Australia

We grow back.
Like eyelashes,
Like fingernails.
Even when we think we are done,
We grow back.
Even after the loss,
Even after the burn,
Our skin heals over.
A little bit stronger,
A little bit smarter,
A little bit softer.
And if you're really lucky
You crawl out with a scar.
Let it be your best friend,
The one who always calls back.
The one who has a spare key.
The one who sends a text just to tell you
That we grow back.
We always grow back.

A Wooden Bench For Two
Emily Gierlich, West Bend, WI

I would have untangled the balls of yarn that make up your mind
Unraveled them down long hallways
And through the desolate, dusty streets of ancient cities

I would have called for you through locked doors with hoarse reverberation
Or slipped crumpled notes underneath them

I would have smoothed your hair and straightened your collar;
Held your hand, coaxed the loneliness from your laughter

I would have sat with you longer with your head on my chest if I had known
what love looked like.

Watch the interplay of memories and longing

How we should have sat in a photobooth
with smiling cheeks pressed together
Happy to contort into the same frame

The opportunity for
six snapshots
that the shutter condemned
as the bulb refused to flash

A set of crushed shadows to hang on my refrigerator

Heckler
Partridge Boswell, Woodstock, VT

—after Anaïs Nin

And naturally I had no choice but to holler Hey, you in the back!
Then the whole audience woke & cringed. So I focused: No not you,
the one beside you who thinks he's not cracked like the rest of us. To-
day is your lucky day! I hate to break it to you, especially since you

came here to dissipate in the crowd. Don't take it too hard, but
when surfaces craze, chances are their truth aches to amaze us.
The last cracks I saw like that, hands chalked them to lower the
risk of slipping. No doubt you assumed you were safe back there

to chill with the shy kids and slackers—you'd just phone-surf and
remain semi-conscious without getting called on or out, hanging
tight with the silence. But hey, now's your shot to have your say
in public and tweet it too—cast off and sing in your sinking—

a chance to join the leaky boats of our stories full of holes! Listen
bud don't expect your neighbor next to you to save you. This rift
was no one's fault line but your own, a mirror won't tell you any
more than a blackmailed sycophant. Only you know where it got

painful as it shroomed into every dark room of you more predictably than a Marvel script, awaiting the day you'd crack wide open and let the light shine in undimmed. What's that? You've heard that old asterisk lyric before—some crackpot troubadour in a black fedora?

It must be true then. Forget the stitches and glue, that stuff dentists took hours shellacking your teeth with: it's a war you can't win or lose. To reiterate, here's a hammer—you know what to do (& btdubs, that blossom of light inside you? It needs a way to get out too).

Landscape in Monochrome No. 1
Alex Ford, New York, NY

the lake a Crème brûlée, ice-crusted, snow-dusted
       flat and white, all flat and white
but for the black teaspoon pool
       carved out of the flat white and flat and white
and the two swans floating headless
       in the black interruption of the wide fat white, so flat the light
the way clouds hover on the surface of the night
       white interruptions of the black so bright
long alien necks and black-trimmed beaks
deleted by the surface of the water opaque and hard
       obsidian mirror too black for sight, reflecting back the night
       an aberration in the flat and white
bare arms of birches splayed spasmodically,
the stripped sycamore spindles grasping up
       with barky fingers long and white,
       fingers stark and straining tight
       reaching into the black night, the lack of light
and the ashes bending low,
almost to scrape the powdered snow

branches bowed like souls contrite
under the weight of meaty white
weighty might
wet bark black as backless night
with clouds upon it floating light
swans with necks, birch branches bright
below the mirrored depthless height
out of sight
pierces flat and endless white
with voided timeless lack of light
and all of it so still.

The Marble's Lament for David
David Ross, Farmington Hills, MI

In Carrara's embrace, I once lay free,
A slab of marble, untouched, content to be.
The earth's cool touch was all I knew,
In Tuscany's quarries, where skies were blue.
Unburdened by artistry, unshaped by hand,
I thrived as marble in my native land.
A piece of the Earth, part of the clay,
Unaltered by chisel, I wished to stay.
Then came Michelangelo, with vision keen,
A sculptor's dream, a creator's scheme.
He saw in my grain a form to birth,
A masterpiece destined for worldly worth.
But I, the marble, in quiet repose,
Was content as I was, nobody knows.
The chipping began, the hammer's dance,
A transformation forced, a new circumstance.
For others' eyes, I was shaped and hewed,
A labor of love, to be understood.
But deep within, I couldn't deny,
A longing for Carrara's open sky.
The sculptor's touch, though skilled and true,
Molded me into something new.
A figure emerged, a man so fair,
Yet I felt a loss I couldn't bear.
The chisel marked changes, both deep and wide,
While I yearned for the quarry's quiet stride.
I became David, a work of art,

But within my core, I felt torn apart.
The world marveled at my sculpted form,
While I yearned for the quarries, the tranquil norm.
Gawked at and praised, I stood on display,
In the Galleria dell 'Accademia, I stay.
But I don't recognize the figure I've become,
A masterpiece, yes, but I feel so numb.
Stripped of my essence, my earthy core,
I stand here alone, forevermore.
Longing for Tuscany's embrace once more,
To be marble again, just as before.
A simple slab, free in the breeze,
Not a statue of fame that the world sees.
I miss the quarries, the rugged terrain,
Where I was whole, where I felt no pain.
Among the hills, under the sun's embrace,
I was complete, a part of that sacred space.
Now I'm David, admired and adored,
But I miss being me, the marble ignored.
A monument to art, a marvel of might,
Yet I yearn for the freedom of the quarry's light.
In the hush of night, I ponder and roam,
A statue on display, yet far from home.
Oh, Carrara's quarries, how I miss your grace,
For there, as marble, I truly had a place.

ECOSYSTEM DISRUPTION - as a haibun
Sheila Bonenberger, Branford, CT

I've been watching the boxy building grow taller and wider replacing phragmites, muddled wetlands. I'll admit, the sluggish stream with its muddy, trash strewn banks bothered me even as building meant displacing birds, insects,

air.   I wanted to straighten tangled branches, snip the choking vines from trees, take a rake to the crackling undergrowth and make it neater, squared away, as if, in some way, that would help me breathe self into alignment with self, but I resist the impulse when it seeps into my thoughts fresh from some anxiety steeped reservoir nourishing a need to force the round

earth   into a cube, even knowing there's life in and under decaying leaves and fallen logs teeming with beetles, wood now so damp and porous it couldn't catch

fire.   Once I saw a mother duck swim out from beneath the bridge crossing this stream. Leaning over the guard rail, I counted four ducklings swimming behind her as she led them between a Styrofoam cup, some soggy match sticks that hissed going in and what resembled a stranger watching me from under water.   Ripples distorted the face I recognized as my own, undulating, reflected in the stream that trickles along like tears under the bridge. Ducks disappear under a weeping willow, past the new building, through the bright green lawn while trucks carrying lumber roar by—

water meanders
trickles into the salt marsh
bleeding out to sea.

Haiku Of Loss
Barbara Dalke, Aurora, CO

Heavy thoughts, so stuck
Wallowed muck sinking lower
Just another day

Drowning tears, so wet
No more big hugs and "love you"
Just another day

Swollen head, so stuffed
Full of blurry memories
Just another day

Sharp pain, so pointed
Jabbed deflated and squashed flat
Just another day

Dull ache, so empty
Silent flashbacks all swirling
Just another day

False front, so hidden
Not really another day
Just pretend it is

Where is my neighborhood?
Katarina Serrano, Denver, CO

Where is my neighborhood?
The place that I had grown?
The street still has the same name,
But this is no place I've known.

That corner store we used to visit
On the end of our block,
Has been torn down and replaced,
With something else now in its spot.

People come and go,
like the seasons in a year.
But what's the point of coming home,
when none of it is here.

I assume my neighborhood was just out of fashion.
Maybe out-dated, or perhaps unkept.
The updated homes are nice and shiny,
But it's the culture that has left.

Anorexia Wins
Vicki Moore, Valles Mines, MO

Looking once more through glass walls,
covered in a waterfall like rain,
distorting the world into curves;
images of unreality from a child's nightmare.
Her bare feet are cold on marble floors;
their blue grey color matching her feet and ankles,
winding its way up paper thin legs.
Veins stand out like blue worms wiggling.
Alone and naked she sits, knees drawn up,
shoulder bones jutting out like gargoyle wings.
Imitating a bird skeleton, soft flesh disappearing,
thin hair dropping on the floor,
like a snake shedding its skin.
Looking in the mirror, she wonders why she is still so fat
as she draws the razor through her bony wrist.

Poetry
Mel Magers, Cave Creek, AZ

Capture a scene

A thought

An emotion

Expose it to the film of the soul

Develop slowly in the darkroom of the mind

Printed on pages of passion

Creating a picture of ageless delight

This is poetry

Sinkside Meditation
Kristen Walton, Honeyville, UT

At day's end, I sit on a stool sinkside,
 Too drained to drain on my feet–
 Another birthday come and gone–
 Another cake made for self
 Because of my need to control everything,
 Right down to how many tablespoons of cocoa are considered chocolatey
 Enough

Each year collected
 Piles up like laundry in the corner,
 Growing only out of sight
 Like weeds multiplying as I sleep in the early hours,
 Bringing a quick intake of breath with each visit I make
 To the garden

These musings are musings alone–
 Awarenesses of my unawareness
 And reflections on impermanence
 Merely existing without judgment–
 Flitting by as I watch the suds whirl,
 Arrogantly supposing that I might have this same sinkside meditation

Once again tomorrow or next week.

Alas, Emma Lazarus!
Jude Luttrell Bradley, Long Beach, CA

Ferryboat crosses historic Hudson River
same one indigenous Lenape1 called "river that flows both ways"
until Dutch thugs gentrified the 'hood, colonial path to blaze.
Stumbled on a world off course from the India shortcut they failed to deliver,
newcomers claimed, renamed, and prefixed everything, as *New* name givers:
christened New Amsterdam, New York, New Jersey, then resident re-
fuse displaced, uppity locals relocated, their homeland seized by treaties
penned in disgrace! Careless colonizers disenfranchised native people –
selling them down the river. River still flows, colossal French girl wading
murky harbor seems out-of-date so-called Mother of Exiles, lanky pati-
nated arm upraised, torch in hand, illuminating promises broken and
buried inside pedestal beneath her feet.
No golden door near statuary grand, hollow monitor of wicked secrets
we keep, of history we misunderstand.

1 A nomadic people belonging to the Algonquin language family, the Lenape
preceded the late 17th century European settlement of New York, New Jersey,
and Pennsylvania by centuries.

Questions for the Troll
Margaret McDermott, Ghent, NY

He lives under the bridge by the freeway,

a brittle, grey cement salon his encampment

A black leather overcoat covers him, even in summer heat

His skin is leather too, like a cowboy taking the long ride

through a mountain pass, months away from a hot bath

I walk by there on Wednesday mornings calling out Hello!

Slow going at first, his eyes merely looking

But I kept on and learned his name is Lawrence

Not Larry? I ask

No, his mother did not like that nickname

How long have you lived under the bridge?

For a while, he said

There is a far away quality about him

Halfway between worlds,

his light blue eyes try their best to blend in with the sky.

Did you grow up around here?

No, I am from somewhere else is all he will reveal

Is there anything I can bring you? He is quiet - thinking

I could use a can opener, he says.

I bring the can opener the following Wednesday,

along with canned goods and a folded-up twenty

When I see him, he has a small black and white dog

Who's this I say? This is Jesus, he says without irony
Does he bite, I ask? No, he laughs, he's friendly
I pet Jesus, who indeed, seems like a good dog
Where'd you find him, I ask?
He found me, Lawrence said.
I was sleeping and he woke me, he was licking my face,
I think he thought I was dead!
His laughter boomed out, echoing under the bridge
Jesus found me, he smiled
I had no further questions that day

BIRD

Story Keatley, Fort Worth, TX

Found something good along the way
Headed to my dread today.
While sorting words I'd not yet heard
My ear was tilted by a bird.
I turned my head to find the sound
And there he floundered on the ground;
Bird looked at me,
And I at he.

Bird said "while I'm not skilled to fly
An unexpected wind came by.
I clung to straws and did my best
But I was scoured from my nest."
His struggles lacked the crisp precision
Honed by wise and worn decisions;
I could not leave
Him there to grieve.

"Let me help." I quietly asked
Then gently took him in my grasp.
Bird could not fight the howling wrath
That flung him squarely in my path.
I reached the nest that reigned above
Tucked Bird in and left my glove,
To keep him warm
and shield from harm.
I turned to face again my dread

But found I pondered Bird instead.
Did he fear wind before he saw;
Before it flung him from his straw?
Odds are, Bird fills the sky with song,
With faith that, should the wind blow strong,
There'll always be
Something like me.

I want to be like Bird

Ashes
Susan Zwingli, Boise, ID

Today, I released your ashes;
the river water rushed to meet them with a holy kiss
as though to rob them from the wind.
I'd heard that some ashes always come back on the thrower
and they did,
shimmering in the sunlight and then
a dusty embrace,
acrid to the eyes and tongue,
powdering my skin,
before dissolving, some twisting into air and others
falling on speckled river rocks in the glacial darting waters.
I felt your molecules in my hair
where your fingers used to weave a pattern,
moving slow and lazy like all the time we thought we'd have.
As the air settled, there you were all around
and the distant humidity of your life…
just there,
but now always out of reach.
No matter how warm the sun on my back,
I couldn't mistake it for one last hug from you.
I lost that long ago.
I know you watched me from where you are
as I wiped the streaks from my face
before setting my shoulders and climbing up the bank.
We know today wasn't for you but for me…
a sacrament of freedom
from the envelope of grief I've traveled in,
a calling to turn my face toward other bubbling streams
and receive what life has yet to give.

Native Son
Luke Benjamin, Denver, CO

I want to know what you left me, native son
where sandstone plateaus burn in the sun.

where alpine peaks buckle down to jagged shale,
and headwaters rush past moss-covered banks
down steppes, and foothills, towards grassy front ranges,
and endless lowland plains.

South southwest wide rivers run, native son
where muddy waters drain into wide floodplain basins,
and silty mangrove estuaries.

where white dunes erode in ocean salt spray
and sand, in the offshore wind, stings your face
as you dive under the waves, eyes closed,
and listen to the whitewater break.

You left me something, native son
where thunderheads eclipse the late afternoon sun
and sagebrush meadows flush green after summer rain
and flickers of cottonwoods and cattails are overlain
with your shadow, as your feet sink in cool river clay.

Denied Access To Fly
Kache' Attyana Mumford, New York, NY

My hands wrap around your bracelet
The one that became mine the night-
You decided to take your life

I want to protect it
But I feel it breaking-
Underneath the pressure of my fingertips

As my belly grows wild
Screaming like a hungry child
As the blame piles

Who told you that you didn't matter
Who told you that you could just end your chapter in the middle of a sentence
Stripping off a glorious story until all that's left is the bare bones of disaster

Who told you to come into my room an hour before
To tell me you loved me - allowing your words to hang on the frame of
my door
Only for you to go and break my heart some more

You wrote that now it would be easier to breathe
But how did you ever expect me to find peace-
After watching you leave

Why didn't you take me?
We were always one heartbeat
And now my heart is stuck on repeat

I hope you're as happy as you thought you'd be
It's the only thing that gives me relief
Truth be told that's a lie - but it's something I need to believe so my lungs
don't forget
how to breathe

Because my love for you outweighs the hate
Of everything you put me through
So I dream of the heaven you once promised me we'd go to

As I wait for death to take me too
I'm sorry I'm not as eager as you

Whisper My Name To The Wind
Samantha Shelton, Blue Springs, MO

The bends in the road help us
dodge the bullet barreling past.
We've gotten pretty good at this.
Breaking our backs. Turning a
blind eye to the obvious. An
unspoken agreement that
we feign ignorance to

Today you take the turns extra slow. While you
focus on the road I'll focus on
counting your hurricane wave eyelashes,
or calculating the degree at which the crescent moon corners
of your mouth curl into a smile, or
following the pattern of your constellation freckles.
I'll ride upside down through your roller coaster hair.
Slide all the way down to your Mount Everest
calloused palms. Engrave every inch of you to memory;
Soon that is all I'll have left

When we reach the end of the road
you hold me longer than you did yesterday
but I continue to play pretend,
plant a "see you tomorrow" kiss
on your cheek. I do not look back when I wave,
but I watch you drive away through the window

When the last of the dust settles,
shards of my heart replace its spot in the wind.

So until I see you again,
I'll sleep with one pillow under my leg,
another in my arms,
and forget that it's not you.
For a split second, I swear
I can feel your breath ruffle my hair.
You whisper my name to the wind

Firewater

Jackie McKenna, New York, NY

The inexorable expectations of
A mid-season Saturday is enough
To stir even him. Knuckling for his snuff,
Bumming a smile, a scent of foxglove
Still on his collar, he falters into
The night. The kind Eliot wrote about,
To sing his *own* love song, off-key, o'er stout,
Or port, or hooch. Perhaps he'll pilfer one for you.
Maybe he'll dance the galliard, kiss
You neath the strobing constellations and
Beckon you into the toilet to piss.
A self-anointed Byron. A firebrand.
A king in his cups, ruling the realms 'tween
Club and ER, tilting just short of windmills.

What will Turn my head Back at the Pearly Gates
Karla k Morton, Raton, NM

There were those 3 minutes, 50 seconds
Willie Nelson singing Stardust
Dancing in socks in the dining room —
hardwood floor space just wide enough
for a sway
Body to body
Hand in hand
Toes, now and then, on toes.

Mom
Brian Eddelson, Garden City, NY

why does a flower bloom
between two slabs of concrete?

maybe soil was brushed
from a passing street sweeper
maybe air conditioners dripped water from above
like industrial rain clouds
maybe sunshine splintered skyscrapers or the hot breath of a bagel store
helped keep the morning frost at bay

maybe it was none of those things

why does a flower bloom
between two slabs of concrete?

maybe she was never meant for a meadow
surrounded by her likeness
to be lost without purpose
invisible
maybe she was meant to exist
in this unfortunate space
to be the yellow amongst the gray
where nothingness thrives
so we can always remember

she rose

and when her time nears
a stiff wind will blow, she will finally succumb
but not before it carries her seed
to another

who learned to be just like her

ten father prophecies
Sarah Saltiel, Providence, RI

1. this is not freudian

2. i promise you, this isn't freudian

3. you shouldn't believe me on that, freud wouldn't

4. keep an eye out for phallic imagery, oedipal eye-gouging, children with wolves as fathers

5. daughter– i, gouged –nineteen sits on a cot in the er, burned,
      acid-caught,
              stomach-dropped,
      calls her father, he takes two hours to show up, stays fifteen minutes, she does not see him again
      for three weeks.

6. daughter, caught,
acid-dropped burns her knees, she needs/ careens/ nineteen, into the er, calls her father,
      he asks her *does it hurt? can it wait?*

7. acid-blooded daughter takes water in her veins and what did he see in those fifteen minutes
that he could not stay, and where did he go and who did he see and did he fray, did he fray like loose
      threads in a rope uncoiling/ roiling–

8. daughter sits caught in the er, on prophecy's word, father swallows her whole.

9. daughter shower-sits with gripped-white-handed nameless nurse
watering skin like something might grow,
like flowers? like grass? like roots? in volcanic ash
      in burn-red body cracked, she wolf-wails

10. daughter, acid-bound

blooded

burned

calls her father, on prophecy's word, he sacrifices her to the sea
serpent, turns to stone when he

sees, she screams, something growing around the knees,

she skin-slips into something else, word other than daughter,
word like bird or volcano or wolf or sea
serpent, she streams into other being entirely, walks home alone in the
New York streets,

sun-roots cracking

through

and through

and through her knees.

Comfort To Our Souls
Deborah Stewart Chinn, Torrance, CA

If all the stars should fade tonight
Who but the sky would know?
Each magic glowing measured light
Might have someplace to go…

If tomorrow's sun forgot to rise
The morning still would come;
It would be easier on the eyes
Perhaps preferred by some…

Should every bloom across the world
Hold a nature strike;
And choose instead not to unfurl
No rose would be in sight…

If every heart would open wide
Let all who pass come in;
No doubt there's room enough inside
Rejoice in your new friends!

But time does strange things to us all
We grow harder through the years;
Our ears refuse to heed the call
Of desperate, pleading tears…

I beg the stars to shine tonight
And the sunlight to rise and glow;
These gifts bring solace and delight
Some comfort to our souls…

The Art of Grief
Rick Ackerly, Belvedere, CA

The air is clean sheets, my rocking chair still.
A pigmy owl comes to perch on the porch
rising moon staring full on through the firs.

I sit with grief.
I mother it,
holding its little hot hand.
I don't say *Shhh*.
I don't say *It's okay*.
I wait until it's done with having feelings,
then we stand and go wash dishes.

Cracking the bedroom doors,
stepping over creaky boards,
we kiss the children,
feeling sore like getting back
from climbing mountains,
training for a marathon.

I'm with you all the way,
whispers my grief.

Then, splashing water on our face,
we stretch beneath the moonlight
one big shadow, one small.

On Bliss
Valerie Dunn, Little Rock, AR

A couple
elderly and deaf
were fitted with hearing aids
for the very first time
It was in the early days of its invention
They longed to hear the music of the earth
Joy and excitement marked the day

But then, they never knew
hard snow crunches so loudly
beneath the feet
Or of the incessant chirp and chatter of the birds
Nor the insufferable honking of the geese
that once used to just sail by

Knew not the ticking of the clocks
or that every light switch clicks and clacks
Knew not the creaking of the floors
Or the jolt from banging doors

Once the novelty wore off
they acknowledged to each other
with a glance
preferring the familiar calm of silence

Hearing aids removed
and gently packed away
somewhere
at the back of a drawer
forgotten

The Pen
Sophia Reji, Broomall PA

The ballpoint pen,
navy blue ink, cushion grip in the same color,
a forgotten local business's logo half gone,
catching when retracting, the clicker worn from hundreds of uses,
it glides across the page smooth and precise every time.
The same pen, you stole from the restaurant on our first date,
slipping it casually into the pocket of your blazer,
refusing to leave a tip.
We had eaten like kings that night.

Your blazer still hangs in my coat closet, hinges loose,
hanging above my burgundy stilettos - scuffed, one heel dangling.
The same stilettos I wore on our fifth date,
when you hurled the pen in my direction.
The scar on my forehead entirely faded.
Your golf clubs are in the closet too, except the one you kept under our bed
on your side,
the one you didn't golf with.

Your remnants are everywhere
whiskey stones, a belt frayed on one end, a swiss army knife,
the teddy bear you gifted me, one eye missing
a punching bag and boxing gloves,
unused, unopen, unscathed.
The ice packs in the freezer.

The cracked sliding door, where your head hit the glass,
the broken railing outside, from where I told them you fell.

The pen lays on the counter now, next to a spiralbound notebook
I'll fix the cracks and breaks,
and clear out your things soon.
First, I'll use this pen to write your final parting words,
a note I'll say, I found amongst your things.

Once it's done,

the rest will go,

but the pen,

it will stay.

My Never Daughter
Lily Nason, Vaucluse, Australia

My never daughter counts the cars
From behind the stained glass
Her face chopped up into fragments
One eye turned green   One cheek turned red
        The teeth of her gappy smile
Splattered across the colours
                In a carnivorous kaleidoscope

                                        Stay with me.

Car watching is nothing banal
On a mundane Monday
She is bewilderment.

I watch her dance
And mouth the beats
        5 6 7 8
her Rond de jambe draws with her feet
an eddy, a Plunge pool.
The floor turns to water and sinks her down and below
As the ice seals itself over her head
She is lost beneath the snow.

                                Don't open your eyes.

She bangs up against the freeze
But all she makes are cracks
of the wrinkles she will never cast

                                        Don't get distracted.

No, my never daughter loves to swim
And so her new habitat, she adores
She beguiles me as she dives deeper down past the sea floor.
bio-luminescence shines from her eyes
And they guide her through the depths
They are blue,
like mine.

                                        Don't wake up

I can't stop it now, my ontology calls
This surreality remains a pyrrhic victory
As light cracks through the door
I have to rise now
Make a cup of tea. Rise up-

                                        Or you'll lose me

Chemo on My Mind
Laura Popovici, Goodyear, AZ

Alcohol pad
wipe wipe.
Out comes
the needle
poke poke.
It finds a vein
flow flow.
The medicine
burns through
my veins
burn burn.
Burning in
my forearm
burning burning.
I want to scream
pull the IV out
pull pull.
Medicine
the doctor
tells me
to save
my life
he says
save save.
But oh -
how it burns
badly badly.
I'm going
out of
my mind with
pain pain.

The Map
Joanna Hoffman, Houston, TX

Some days, hate slithers through
the screen and an icy fear cobras
around my throat. Some days
even the dawn is straitjacketed
in despair's stubborn jaws.
What can I do but
pray my heart into a bell
peeling off the paint chips of night
with a song sharp as needlepoint.
Nothing is promised and that is both
a nightmare and a dream. Some nights
all I can do is lay awake listening
to the soft pendulum of her breath.
Some nights I seance all the ghosts I love
to hold my empty hand in the dark.
I can't swallow the misery that swirls
around the headlines, the email subjects,
the laughing emoji on a Facebook post
about someone's heartbreak. All I can do is
stand at the canyon's edge and scream. All
I can do is lean forward to the screen and
close my eyes, let the ache in my chest be
the sonar stitching the map that will lead
me forward, where the trees tangle together
and we don't need roads.

My Therapist Says Smiling More Will Help Me
Adrian Potter, Minnetonka, MN

unwrap the blanket of indifference that has swaddled me
since birth. But explain that to the gravity pulling my spirits

downward and grounding my aspirations like planes in need
of repair, or mention that to the doubt loitering in my mind

like a ghost in a basement, restless and haunted by this new,
hollow habit of falsely flashing teeth. No one got the memo

that shedding my resting scowl would hypothetically shine
a low-watt light onto the dim confines of my inner thoughts

as God sews dusk into darkness, which, too, remains stitched
to the aesthetic of my nocturnal soul as it stirs like a compass

needle seeking the right direction. People claim I can cure
this contagion, that depression will surrender its weapons

and retreat limber-tailed back to the hell that spawned it,
but I know of no devil who would willingly banish itself

without invoking turmoil as part of its exit strategy. And still,
on the days I do savor life, the sunrise leaves me stunned

like a random hello from a cranky neighbor who usually cares
less. On the days I do savor life, I hope the fog of the past

lifts and gives way to clearer vision, so I can finally see
how flowers bloom even in times of despair. Every day

above ground should be cherished, so my mouth becomes
a closed casket for the complaints that die inside it, unsaid,

despite their yearning to be resurrected and uttered. I get
so enlightened that I glow in the dark. I ache for happiness

to etch itself in black and white, but remain disappointed
as it arrives uncertain and grey, synthetic as my forced smile.

My Mother the Raft Builder
Lola Cooper, Everton Park, Australia

My mother built a raft on the ocean we used to live in.
She built it out of blue card envelopes and expired passports and Ikea instruction manuals, New car smell
and nail polish painted house keys, Exposure therapy, and live music and "let me pay for that"
Adhesive made out of moving box tape, suitcase locks, menstrual pads, sweat, and tears

She uses cigarette smoke and unopened champagne bottles to keep it afloat
Old pictures are tossed to make room for bus routes, toll roads, and the address of the illegal tobacconist
The boat is filled with hope wearing a dog collar, but somehow it is the ashes of a cat that weigh the most
A flag made of white baby clothes flies in the breeze, held up by a mast made from the wood of a cabinet
recovered from an old storage shed and the melted, mangled plastic of old Barbie dolls
It seems to tell all the other ships *I surrender the memories, come take them*
We never get visitors.

My mother is the captain. Her job is keeping a vessel afloat whose job is to sink.
By that, I mean she is my mother.
She asks me for "sorry" in Mandarin and Korean and Spanish as if language can fill the holes.
I crochet plugs made of rainbow loom bands, I weave report cards and college acceptance letters

We sometimes use our appendages to fill the holes, and secretly we hope the holes will take us with them
We look for old furniture and books to stop the leaks and realise they didn't rise to the surface with us

She complains - rightfully- about the seasickness,
and the shoddy crew mates - the ones who have lived on the raft their entire life
The same ones who ask her "if the ocean is so much better why did you leave?"
And "If the sea was so cruel, why do you long to go back?"
Our dehydrated, sleep-deprived hallucinations involve throwing them all overboard.
Instead, we learn that responding is as easy as laughing.
Which is to say it isn't easy at all, but we do it anyway.

On nights when the tears drip down my mother's face like rain rolling off a window, she says
"I took you from the fluorescent jellyfish,
from dolphins, and sparkling sea shells.
Even the angler fish with their sharp teeth were something compelling.
on the raft, there are so many seagulls who poke you and steal your shiny things.
I took you from an ocean you could dream to the bottom of, and rise to the top of."
I don't know how to tell her that those things are only lovely when you don't have an anchor tied to your ankle

So every time she tells me how sorry she is that we live on a boat,
I try to tell her I'm glad I don't have to pretend to breathe seawater anymore
That sunburn hurts again and again and again, but the sky is so much bluer than the water ever was.
That you can only be grateful for the beauty of the ocean when you're not drowning in it

Lifeguarding
Kate Levin, Los Angeles, CA

The local mom who cupped my cheeks
in her hands at my mom's funeral
and sobbed, *Whatever you need*
gives me my first summer job
at sixteen. A gym teacher with
two sons at my school, she runs
the town pool like a Marine
on speed. Opening day, she flings
to each girl guard a Speedo
of the same tiny size. Climbing up
to the chair, I don't know how I arrived
at a life so ill-fitting. All I do is squint
into unsuitable futures. A thick blankness
everywhere. In the water below me
figures swirl and blur beneath the glare.

One thing they teach you in lifeguard class:
drowning doesn't look like drowning.
The swimmer doesn't flail, they fall,
slipping beneath the surface without a yell
or splash. If you look for thrashing, you'll
miss the quiet sinking. The winter she

retreated to her room for good, I stood
sentry outside my mother's door without
knowing what I was watching for. Just blind
dread: was the threat coming from the world
or from the tomb she'd made of her bed?
I didn't know, and I couldn't dive in.
Those months she lived on nicotine
and tea, she would emerge without a word
to fill her cup. One day she stopped cleaning
the sugar she spilled in the kitchen.
A sticky pool of crystals glittering
on the counter. A river of ants lining up.

Dragonfly Deities
Leah Dreyer, Appleton, WI

I have discovered the reason for existence
in the color of dragonfly wings
as they ghost over the edge of the water's mirror
with speckles of sunlight and all the rainbows hidden in the breeze,
lapping over the tips of their gossamer coats.
They wear their violet flakes with all the nobility their station demands,
and the fire's breath for whom they're named sparks over those wings.

There is a deity in their veins.
The dark lines composing a hymn
whose melody sounds in the gentle buzz and hum of flight,
and in their eyes reflect all the worlds that have already decomposed
over countless years of nonexistence.
There is an infinite eternity of possibilities that they see
that I can only imagine,
and the only god I've ever cried to rests upon their slim bodies,
cradled in arms too small to hold so many dreams.
And I wonder if they fly high enough,
will they reach the sun and leave behind this world of sorrow
just as all the other gods before them have done?
Until we are left coughing blood as we cry their names aloud,
wondering how foolish mortal men can be
to scream themselves hoarse for a god that never cared,
and maybe that is always destined to be the end of deities.

But for now,
I watch in silent awe
in the stillness of the summer sun
as I see myself reflected in the gleams of dragonfly wings,
as great as any knight in a tale of old,
conquering the beast,
being crowned a king,
becoming a god.

dear mol.
Mercy Haub, Shoreline, WA

Please stop.
Stop sneaking into my dreams, lurking behind every door and plotline.
Stop showing up in my photo memories, "One year ago today".
Stop echoing in my thoughts, my observations. Stop injecting adrenaline and anxiety into my entire body at every crumb of correlation.

Now that you're gone, I see how clearly poisoned parts of our past were. You played with my mind and my habits and I can never forgive you. I hate you for what you did. I hate anyone who does what you did and somehow you doing it made it worse.

My lungs seem deeper, my mind doesn't reel trying to steer the conversation away from things I don't want to do Or decipher your references or secret undertones, my heart saved from the cycle of reliance and rescue.

But. I miss you, too.
I don't want to speak to you so I am writing this, to tell you how much you linger.

I wondered if, after time, it would all reveal itself to be superficial, a tattoo that was constantly around, constantly visible, But sat only on the top layer of skin, never seeing bone or blood. Skin takes on attackers that the heart never knows, but the heart struggles with the weight of the world. And I didn't expect you to have inked your way down there. But you did.

We'd talk about sleepless nights, reliving the past from every angle, every fear echoing louder in our minds' chambers. At first, you jumped out at me every night after my eyes shut, chasing after an explanation, forcing a conversation, Manipulating the storyline and my responses, accusing me of tricking the world, you, myself, That instead our relationship was a facade, something easily broken and forgotten. Truth be told, very few things could have broken our friendship, and you decided to seek them out.

I would wake up with my heart in my throat, gagging on the idea of seeing you again, knowing I would choke on my words And betray my intentions.

Just when I started to sleep through the night,
I'd get a new bag of mangos, a photo would pop up, I'd paint my nails, we'd order Thai, my prescription would get a refill, My sister would ask about you.

Hope would ask about you.

Do you know how much it broke my heart to tell her that we don't talk anymore and explain why without truly telling her?

I hate how much of me is related to memories of you. I look back and see how you inserted yourself in everything. It was nice to have a constant, even if you were the embodiment of the opposite. I know my mind better because of you and I hate how much we would say we had the same brain.

I hold onto endless reservoirs of our memories and it hurts so much because I love and treasure each one. I keep some of them in my core, using them to hold myself up and keeping them from the poison of my mind. They are that special.

I wonder how you are right now sometimes, but mostly I wonder who I would be right now without you.

I think I survived the parts of you that clung and obstructed like the sticky slides and cigarette butts at a grungy, forgotten playground, Which makes it harder to disregard the childlike playfulness and wonder and care that coated many of our interactions.

I do not regret the distance, space, avoidance.
I do regret the things we learned together, because they hold too much power and I'm glad they happened.
I did not expect this to be this hard.

I know hate is such a gift of an emotion, so uncomplicated most times: pure anger and hurt, vengeful and gone. Hating you gives you more power over me and means that my dreams will forever hold a place for you, warping even the ease of that emotion.

Please be done. I am. We are.
Leave me be.

Willing To Fall
Bella Wright, Mead, CO

the best things in life are waiting in a place one step down from a ledge,

disguised as a towering cliff,

so that they are sure the only people that get to enjoy them

are the people willing to take the jump,

and most importantly,

are willing to fall.

Stress Eater
Shonda Buchanan, Playa del Rey, CA

The Washington Post's Aug. 14, 2023
headline said, "Brains and other body parts,
mostly from people of color,
were taken without consent."

And I heard clearly in my brain,
I'm going to stress eat right now.

Article said, "Smithsonian's collection
of human remains is one of the largest in the world;
its collection of 255 brains were taken
mostly from Black, Indigenous people
and other people of color."

My mind said, *go eat some more.*
And I ran to the kitchen to eat and eat and eat
even though I'd had breakfast
stuffed my face with crackers and cheese, humming,
don't cry, don't cry, but the water came anyway.
And as tears fell, I ate those too.

Caption murmured,
"Brains were collected to further racist theories"

I eat some more.
Eating the trauma, eating the fear,
eating the knowledge of the absence of Black brains
from Black bodies.
I eat for the hunger of Black slaves.
For Sarah. For Phillis.
For our brains and body parts hanging
on some marble wall, in basements
under the clean, shiny floors
of institutional buildings
I've paid to visit.

And then, after I'm fuller than I should be,
licking crumbs and sorrow and history from around my mouth,
wrecked, simply wrecked for the rest of my day,
this month, year, decade, this millennium,
I sit down and write this poem

praying to the ghosts of Nat Turner and Wanda Coleman and Hannible
and James Baldwin and Toni Morison and Huey P. Newton
to find those muthafuckas who took our brains from our bodies
and show them what it means to be human.
Or dead.

23

Jashima Brathwaite, Brooklyn, NY

I've hated myself for some time,
But something about 23 feels vibrationally different.

It took some time to get used to,
But I feel more connected.

Re-wired into an upgraded woman.

I used to take a long time to get ready-
Since then,
Nothing else has changed, but the way I view myself.

I have fallen in love with every fold and uniquely placed birthmark.
The broad nose that grew with me through the heckling,
Now adorned with dainty jewels.

The hair that I destroyed trying to look more "presentable",
Sits plumply atop my head.
I've begun to, truly, date her in a way.
Not looking to make her something- or more correctly, someone she's not.

My lips have granted me the opportunity to bestow love upon anyone I
deem worthy.
Speak the experiences my brain kept tucked till the time was right…
And though I wished she was smaller or bigger through the years,
She grew to be the perfect entity.

And the way my skin has braved me through the storm...
I thank God every day for this precious body,
And these features to complement my life.
They tell a story of who I was,
And who I am lucky enough to become.

I've said so many things over the years,
And put so many narratives into my head,
And for once I'm glad that I failed.
I'm just happy to finally be catching up with myself.

This particular life.
From the features,
To the experiences...

This "dress" of sorts.
Still looks great on us,
And it always will.

After Twenty-Two Years I Mistake My Biological Father for a Stranger at Reptile Gardens, A Premier Roadside Tourist Trap
Courtney Huse Wika, Spearfish, SD

It was your girlfriend, now wife, who approached me in the Safari Room,
put her hand on my arm
as I was watching the blue-tailed skink's gummy tongue

snatch the unsuspecting fly.
She was familiar, but I did not recognize
the voice that told me when I was five that cigarettes taste like cherries,

or the hands that poured your drinks at night
and made scrambled eggs when you forgot to buy food for my weekends.
I thought maybe she was a person from work I couldn't place,

and in my Midwest nicety I extended my hand to you, her husband,
and introduced myself. You said,
I know who you are. I am your father

and we were in South Dakota in August surrounded by palm trees,
an African parrot, a manmade pond where the double-crested toads
blinked off-key—
every one of us out of place.

You were much smaller than I remembered, and quieter
when not holding us hostage in your unhappiness: whiskey in your belly,
heart like a fist. You held my hand in yours

and I all I could think about was the sound that wood makes when it splinters,
the way ceramic can never really be glued back together as
tourists, oblivious, brushed past us, hair frizzy and skin sticky in the heat,

their kids decked out in holographic crocodile visors,
patriotic popsicles melting down their wrists
as they chased leopard geckoes around fake boulders.

How much irony before time and space collapse?

On what I thought was the last day I'd see you,
mom and I celebrated at Gator's Pizza in Pierre, ushering in our new life
with stringy mozzarella, the pop and sting of fountain Coke. Now here
you are again,

smile glistening, Maniac the Gigantic Croc grinning
from his neon promotional poster just beyond your shoulder.

Incognito
Eileen Huging, Cowaramup, Australia

I wonder if there will ever be,
A time when I'll feel truly free,
To be myself, be who I am,
Rather than someone who just meets demands.
The expectations others have of me,
Have little to do with my own dreams,
But I must meet my responsibilities
And play the role assigned to me.

Yet within me a silent spirit hides,
An identity that must be denied.
And for this cowardice I must pay,
So in private moments my tears betray,
The emptiness I always feel,
In pretending this mask is real.

For to reveal myself involves such risk,
Empaths and dreamers are just misfits.
This world is no place for vulnerability,
Femininity has been lost as has chivalry.
It's better to have strength and assertiveness,
Than sensitivity and tenderness.
Society only values those qualities,
That are practical, marketable commodities.

So, I'll wear the mask, say "I can cope",
While my ego fights and my spirit hopes
That by some accident of discovery,
Someone special will come to see,
The truth that lies behind the façade,
And hold what's there in high regard.

Intertwined
Ella Lukowiak, Sea Girt, NJ

Dedicated to David Selves, aged 12, who died off Woolich supporting his drown-
ing playfellow and sank with him clasped in his arms on September 12th, 1896

what is it to be known
to have someone stretch their trembling
limbs around your heart
    mason.
the boy turns for his other
lips locked moments before
tumbling through trees sworn to secrecy
their eyes turned to the feather-dotted sky, birds singing their
       songs of indifference
arching their necks to look up, heat flares in their cheeks and arms
the anticipation of palms running down each other's chests
       the boy's heartbeat, beat, beat, beat
it was quiet, the split
a low rumble, like the gurgle in his father's throat
before the bloom of bruises
    mason.
the boy didn't think, didn't breathe, only moved
all inhibition knotted as shivers danced up his spine
at the edge of the slice, the boy heard his name
    david, david, david
electricity bloomed across skin freshly stroked red
he bit his tongue, suffocating a wail
mind running to prayers long ago buried
       fear cleaning locks to doors rusted from negligence

the boy didn't speak, only wrapped his trembling arms around
the small body of his lover
pressing his blueing lips to skin coated in gooseflesh
        he did not flail, he did not swim
but instead prayed for the trees to release their secret
to signal from every branch for a soul to stumble
into their frozen embrace

the boy feels muscles sag above him
and runs his fingers down the limp arms of the boy he loves
steadying his eyes on what is here, what is now
shedding everything but his heart
        still beating, still loving
water bites at his gut, his chest, his hands that refuse
to cease stroking a rigid chest
until the cold flees altogether, fingers pausing
upon the edge of a rib
and the boys feel nothing at all

For My Mother
Lauren Wright, Detroit, MI

Do you ever think about how your mom deserved better?

How the men that claimed to love her, failed in every way?

I wonder if my mom has ever really been in love.

I wonder if any man has ever learned that she loves horror movies, or

the color blue, or the way she feels when warm, salty air washes over her.

I wonder if they know she used to be wild,

And magnificent.

I think about who my mom would have been had she not loved terrible men.

I would not exist.

But, my God, she would.

I imagine her traveling the world.

Making everyone fall in love with her beauty,

Her humor.

She's funny.

She is so funny, but no one is there to laugh at her jokes.

They don't understand her.

And I wonder what I have inherited from her.

I have found love in deserts of men.

Learning to suck out the smallest ounce of affection.

She taught me how to run on fumes.

How to be grateful for any amount of effort.

She taught me how to love.

How to give, and give, and give.

But, I don't know how to take it in

I don't know what it looks like to be loved.

I think I deserved better.

I think I worry for my daughters.

Cella
Rebecca Buckle, Ontario, Canada

Lilies of spiders bloom
In the passage of autumn.
A flower of whispering
Petals paint miles
Of crimson as they
Plague our ending.
Lilies of decease, stems
Of misfortune, fields
Of farewell. A poison
Enchanting, a burning
To the touch. They
Cluster in families but
The lily stands alone.

Bury my body beneath the
Spider lilies. Let my nerves
And veins reach through
Dancing petals and let me
Feel the wind and rain
As I decay. Let me fade
Into the breath of the
Flower of death, and let
Them hold my story until
The end of days.

These Things
Yetta Muse Patterson, Germantown, MD

There is a Dove that coos in the distance.
A waterfall that flows freely into the River Nile.
Who hears it? Who sees it?
There is a father who dances at his daughter's wedding.
A mother who wishes life were better for her child,
walks through frightful times.
Who cares about these things?
Who brought them about?
They are for such a time as this.
There is nothing new under the sun.
When we think something has ended, it has only just begun.
As the days get longer and the years shorter,
remember from whence we have come.
Listen more carefully to the coo of the Dove.
Drink in the waterfalls, if you are so blessed.
Think on these things.
See how the sun rises to mark the start of a New Day.
Light the way, so war turns into peace.
Despite some of these things, taste and see that Life is good.
The grapes on the vine burst with sweetness.
Taste wine that makes the heart glad!
Endeavor to enjoy these things that were designed only for you.
What are these things, you say?
They breathe Life and New Hope.
Tell of these things and lighten the world's burdens.
These Things are of Life!

Expensive
Taylor Melvin, Lynchburg, VA

Love is expensive.
It bears all things,
Things unimaginable until confronted face-to-face.
That which is essential is always expensive,
Purified by the altar fire that burns all else.

Love is expensive.
It does not insist on its own way.
Love trades what is easy for what is best,
Waiting, believing, trusting
For the fruit that it will bear.
And it will bear fruit,
But never in its own way.

Love is expensive.

Dick
Jerry Smaldone, Arvada, Colorado

Dick took a drag off his Marlboro and tried to exhale.
He was sitting on the porch, waiting for the sun to go down,
waiting to die.

He had stage 10 cancer and enough other stuff to kill a horse.
A big 'ol warhorse, more like a workhorse, pulling a wagon,
pulling a plow'. Now it was coming to an end, and he thought
of all he'd done. The farm in Ioway, a stint in the Navy,
the precision of the machine shops, winding bike rides
in the mountains and hunting with his boys.

He was alone now, Rosie gone two years.
He was proud of how he'd cared for her,
The love of his life, unable to breathe.

That first time he walked in the Ramblin' Rose
and saw her behind the bar. How she trusted him,
wanted him in her hard-headed, independent way.

Yeah, he was alone, but the girls, his stepdaughters,
came by to check on him and bring him dinner once in a while.
He had decided to do the right thing and let the family know.
Maybe somebody would want the guns he hadn't used in years,
the bike he couldn't ride, the truck. Somebody'd want the truck.

He thought how he would miss sitting here, watching the
neighbors, young ones pushing trikes and wagons full of
impossibly cute kids, old ones limping around small gardens of
vibrant jewels, some he hardly knew, who'd come by for a casual talk
as word had spread down the block.

He eyes teared up as they rose to the blurry trees and clouds
and everchanging sky. A perfect still life it was, life that is,
with just the right amount of pain and joy to wake you up and
raise you to higher place. And then something lit up inside his
head and he realized that was it.

We had to be lifted up to get to heaven, all of us,
we had to lose this wasted, worn flesh, to see who we really were.
We had to put on a body of shining light to enter the illuminated world.

Dick lit another smoke and took a swig of beer.
The air was clean today, sweet as your first breath.

Grace. And Aches I Didn't Feel a Short Memory Ago
Linda Speranza, Buckeye, AZ

Your skin is delicate, softer than I expected and
your silver hair bounces light like no other color can.
I trace the scar down your chest.
To have found love late in life
makes touching profound.

It was easy once, holding deeply with fire,
without limits.
Now time boldly shows itself,
in a joint that cries,
or as my bones count each year with an ache.

Our bodies are fluid enough to entangle.
Yet sometimes, laughing, we untangle,
rubbing an unexpected ache.
While the longing then weaves us into each other again.

But sometimes, wrapped tightly together,
in a moment of grace, aches are gone,
and the tangle of us lay suspended without time.

Flourish
Aisha Claire Robins, San Antonio, TX

Swollen, squat ovates,
consistent in random conformity,
attest "no water be here" is a lie.

Pimpled and warted, yet lollipop
coronas in lemon, mango, and coral
burst with waggish insolence.

Spiny giants loom, Jacks-in-a-box
big as the sky oblige shadows to
waltz with the sun.

Wind-swept seeds, emissaries to
populate the neighborhood
sprout where they fall. Or not.

Exempt from weather, time-lapse and
no-time-at-all, desert magicians
conjure survival with a flourish.

Numbing of a Nation-State
Matthew Whiton, Littleton, NH

Solicit from thy soulless dreg
Thy curs-ed cultivar, and beg
Your damned pernicious deed
To plague the soil and the seed.

Sickly savored, sweet the sin
Forging fetters kin-to-kin
Shackled shelter, writhing shame
Flirting with a fickle flame.

Vice verboten, salve sublime
Corpse-coercing concubine
Haggard host to tides of time
Future fading in the prime.

Incision licks, precision nil
Tear temperance from hollow will
O vacant vessel, poison pill
Thine ink across the canvas spill.

Punctured prudence, starlight stare
Seek decadence in disrepair
A beast abreast of angel's ire
Cloaked in common man's attire.

Chaos coursing through the cogs
Evoking empty epilogues
Cadaver caucus, rinse repeat
A waltz of wasted misfit meat.

Numbing noxious needle-prick
Lamenting lyric, somber, sick
Cried out across a nation-state
A crux, a crossroad, cast of fate.

Devil dances, dour display
A dogma destined for decay
To wither in his wicked way
Profess to thee your price to pay.

Flick the fingers, clutch the cross
Beseech thy beggar coin a toss
Within the well of dark desire
Fortune's favor is a fire.

I'm Sorry I Can't Be a Coffee Coaster
Amelie Peterson, Trinidad, California

I wish I could say I didn't know from experience
That the boundary I tediously drew
Is the only thing keeping you here

I know you think that you're different from the rest
I'm sorry that makes you just like the rest

I'm only worth earning, only worth having
As long as I'm just out of reach

You only want to know more
As long as something is kept a secret

You only value my vulnerability
If I'm never completely vulnerable

You only want me if you think there's a chance
That if you gave it your best shot, you couldn't earn me

A jigsaw puzzle incomplete is a challenge
A jigsaw puzzle solved is a coaster for a coffee cup
Or maybe just a table ornament

I'm only exciting if I'm not excited
I'm only captivating if I'm not captivated

You'll want to look at me all day
As long as you know that you can look away
Before I catch you looking

I'm sorry that you're not the first, second or third
To hold me only long enough for a selfie–
To care for me only as long as I fit on a bracelet or in a pocket

I'm incapable of allowing myself to be a coaster one more time.
I'll take my chances with going unsolved

Joy
August James, London, England

No joy,
Or hope,
Or laughter,

Be grateful. Snap out of it!

The shadow of depression is suffocating,
a plastic bag pulled tight over my head.

A lonely horizon.
Welcome as an old friend.
Numb, empty, hollow.

Get over it! What's wrong with you!

a fight,
a battle,
Every minute,
every second.

Eventually, you tire.
Depression does not.
The toll too high.
The coins all spent.

I'm sorry, please come back! Please don't leave me all alone.

Dewdrops
Hayden Park, Irvine, CA

"Look, darling, your favorite!"
Mother's voice was slightly strained as she pointed at the painting

The tree was beautiful as always
But not nearly as much as the expression on your face

The tension had gone
And your eyes were closed peacefully
There was a single tear resting on your cheek
Like the roses with dewdrops on the morning you were born

"Darling,"
Mother started but she never finished the sentence
She knew - the silence knew - I knew

The tree in the painting was green, lush with life
I wiped away your tear and said nothing

Mother's presence was warm as always
And I let myself be still

Barnacle Human
Lola Cooper, Everton Park, Australia

"*And What About you?*" they ask finally.
Did you get bored? tongue-tied? Are you fatigued? Don't you love your voice?
Are you saying you could love mine?

This is NOT a poem about love. This is a poem about
      a thing/spectacle/person?
           is there a face in the fantasy? (there is when they talk to me).
Incandescent daydreaming, about consent. why, yes! my standards are declasse.
the bar
      is on the floor. But then again, so am i. falling is, and has always
been, the easy bit. crashing, burning, smiling at messages, sweeping, dy-
ing, loving, tumbling is delicately bittersweet. And thrashing, trying,
fighting, swimming towards light, kicking, suffocating is just
                                              bitter.

And i'm so tired, and the light is so far away, and they don't ever tell you
how warm the embrace of someone who doesn't care is, how easy it is to
writhe in the dark. how you can do anything you want, whenever you
want. because, in truth,
      you might be looking at them but i promise, they aren't looking
at you.

this is NOT a poem about love. it's about blinding blue light, not sleep-
ing even if you wanted
to. it's aching it's unintelligent pining. It's the getting a crumb and giv-
ing a loaf It'sgiving a language and getting a word, and then saying thank
you and meaning it.

It's about not caring at all and caring too much. and its the
waiting and the waiting and the waiting and the waiting and the waiting
and the waiting and the waiting

and then I think i could face it, i could make *them* face it. make them
look me in the eyes and tell me: *i'm sorry.* (~~except, that they wouldn't ever~~
~~say that~~) *no.* ~~(They'd definitely say that)~~
        then this *really* wouldn't be a poem about love.
this illusion is a funhouse: sure i'm dizzy, but i'm still laughing. i am
ignorance's uninvited guest,
i overstayed my welcome by simply showing up and i'm not planning
on leaving.

A reminder that this is NOT a poem about love. It's about making some-
thing out of nothing.
And the *"what about you?"*'s stoking the fire, watering my inhibitions,
holding my hand.
it's never been important-
        tome: i would've stopped this charade to you: it's just me.
the parody script of it all plays on loop a humbled servant, kissing your
feet - after begging to.

look up: synonyms for fine, synonyms for *screaming noises*, synonyms
for forget me - talk about yourself, synonyms for spiderman kissing up-
side down in the rain, looking beautiful but literally
drowning to be with her.
"And what about you?" they ask.   "I'm good"

And I Wonder
Sarah McCormick, Honolulu, HI

I look at you,
this person we created,
and I wonder:
What will you become?

But I am snapped back
into water spilling and velcroing shoes;
into yawning as we snuggle at 2:53 AM
the sun still sleeping but your dreams not coming as easily.

Back into sliding on the playground and
kicking the water as the ocean waves hug your knees -
into hand signs
cries of independence
decoding words
and endless snacks;
into splashing in the collapsible bathtub
and reading upside down,
into
blowing bubbles,
dancing in the living room after dinner,
gentle pats,
and sloppy kisses.

and I wonder:
When will you stop sharing your snacks with the dog?
When will you ride your bike without Dad holding it in balance?
When will you tell me a story?
When will you ask me a question I am not able to answer?

The Wren on Our Front Porch
Jane Marie Law, Ithaca, NY

Hiding motionless
Her nest in our hanging basket
Listening to our chirping
We drink our coffee
Worrying about our children
Hers, yet to hatch
Under her warm, tiny body

We move about
She flies to a branch
Chastising us:
Parents should understand one another better!
Leave me alone
To hatch my eggs and raise my babies in peace

A Trick of the Heart
Jacqueline Gamboa, Chicago, IL

I thought I felt a connection
As you passed by
Like the electricity in the air before a storm hits
But it was just a trick of the wind

I thought I saw love
In your eyes
Speckled like the stars I'd hang in your night sky
But it was just a trick of the moon

I thought I smelled your perfume
On my clothes, lingering throughout the day
Like the sun does on the horizon in the middle of summer
But it was just a trick of the flowers

I thought I tasted forever
I swear it was right there, on the tip of my tongue
Like Ice cream and French fries, savory yet sweet
But it was just a trick of this wine

I thought I heard "I love you"
Spill from your lips, just ever so nonchalantly
Like a scene from a favorite fairytale movie
Where it ends happily ever after
But it was just a trick of the heart

Panther by Moonlight
Damen O'Brien, Queensland, Australia

The panther by my bedroom door
woke me from my sleep with a grunt
or snarl, low husk of invitation. How
did I know that he was a panther?
Sliced out of shadow, cool pelt of night,
a breath of leaves sighing against a window,
and not a tiger or other creature of the
jungles of the mind? Something told me,
wake and look for a panther by your door.
Just once, when I was young and
while my head was still, I saw
a panther stalking by my door, and knew
from the deep certainties of sleep,
that I should not move, until the
merciless moon had carved out its
constant passage, tarred mothwing
hackles, unpacked a tail of shadows
back into its fuming spray of light.
Why was I given a panther?
I do not think I could be as resolute
as those, who for an hour of chance
moonlight are given back their loved ones.
That's an old and bitter curse. But
perhaps when I was young, I was
brave enough to be given a panther.

Where Love Died

Abigail Stallings, Wake Forest, NC

My heart is an abandoned home
Love once dwelled inside
Now I'm left to bury its bones
And drain the ocean I've cried

It started with a broken window
And cracks in the foundation
Until what was broken was beyond repair
As I realized the most my lover would be was complacent

So I threw away the welcome mat
And packed away my things
But I left love to die there
With the empty promises and tarnished rings

Soon the ceiling caved in
The wood began to rot
Over time, it quietly decayed
Now there's nothing but an empty lot

But hope is not lost
For something can be built once more
But this time, I will only settle for a palace
Instead of just four walls and a door

Where My Mind Goes (2006)
Filippo Vanni, New York, NY

The velvet is green and soft
My head
Laying back on the softness
A rain of dust.

Blue and pure, the light.
of an afternoon day
where kids played in the street below
street vendors shouted and sang
Up here, it is quiet.
The structured quietness of golden dust notes
Floating.
And I am floating too.

Forgive Me
Marc Maleri, Shelton, CT

Forgive me
I don't mean to stare
But I've never set my eyes on a beauty so ethereal
Eyes the color blue
Plucked straight from the sea
Lips full and soft
As clouds on a summer's day
Body carved by Michael Angelo himself
I could eternally trace your figure with my hands
Drifting my fingertips along every curve
Of your silky skin

Beneath the flawlessness that is your flesh and bone
Lies a mind so mysteriously winding and intricate
A maze of labyrinthian complexity
That I glady wish to journey into
To lose myself within
I hope to discover every chamber
To walk down every hall of your psyche
To reveal the paths that guide me to your heart

I will gaze upon the cracks
That have been left by past lovers
Learn their stories
Their misdoings
So that I may mend the damage that has been done

I know you hate that I pry
But I beg you to call off the defenses
Be at ease
I do not plan to add any further damage
To a heart that is still beating so strongly and harmoniously
Despite the damage it has been through
Allow me to feel its warmth

Forgive me
I don't mean to stare
But how could I pull my eyes away from my dream incarnate
From my desires brought to life
From the person I was born to love

Firefly
Daniela-Demetrice Stamate, Constanța, Romania

I wonder how primitive creatures lived between the moonlight shadow
and its swing.

I wonder how they felt nature's aura among the fields.

Running freely through the wet grass,

Born to search for wisdom and baptized by the last living ray of sunset.

I wonder what a bond would mean.

I wonder if strength would win against love.

I wonder if they wonder.

I wonder if they still exist...

Cause with thoughts vanished, they are fleshy-slender bodies,

Towering above the sharp peaks fur-lined in the rising mist.

But down there, it's still a frail light,

Ripping away even from the reaper himself, a drop of joy.

His thoughts fade for sadness and grow fiercely for the nobility of love,

While souls fall onto the black,

While other everlasting beings give up and get tired,

Of running with no escaping, addled in that roaring haze.

And as the pitch-dark dusk opens its swan wings,

All the stories scattered in the sky have impressed the selenic queen with
eternal diamonds.

Now the little boy venerates the night of shooting stars,

Even so, his will won't make him a star,

He will end up as a firefly like all the other innocent souls.

But as he ran with dirty human feet to keep up with the hive's game,

He passed through a grave of fireflies,

And washed the greed of the world with one sheer tear of love.

The Window
Julia Griffin, Statesboro, GA

The Valediction Memorial at Prague's main railway station - representing
trains used to transport 669 children from the Czech capital to Britain -
was left with a long crack across the length of a symbolic window pane.

The vandalism appeared to be aimed at disfiguring the shrine's most evoc-
ative feature, a train window engraved with handprints depicting adults
and children forced to say farewell in heartbreaking circumstances.

-The Guardian 10th June 2019

Keep the memorial so: our broken hands,
Hammered and slashed across the finger tips.
We sent our children over murderous lands;
We packed them off and prayed they'd reach the ships.

We crammed *kufriky* - clothes to keep them warm;
Some little, foolish things that saved a fuss.
We wrote short, cheerful notes, in simple form.
We scratched between the lines. Remember us.

We pulled them down the platform to the trains.
We pushed them up the steps. We tried to wave.
Their hands grew smaller on the window panes.
What happened then? They cried, maybe, were brave,

Began forgetting (we could hope) the gash
They'd witnessed in the air. This wound expands,
While all we were is long since baked to ash.
Keep the memorial so. Our broken hands.

The Most Potent Weapon
Amy Haddad, Omaha, NE

Throughout the history of warfare, the simplest, most obvious weapons have often turned the tide of some great battle. Thus, the victim becomes the front line of defense. Upon her vigilance depends the success of science in controlling disease.
– Self-Examination of the Breast. The Cancer Bulletin, 1951, Houston, Tx.

The menace, the threat responsible
for so many deaths, must never be allowed
to advance. At the expense
of no more than a few minutes,
the woman possesses the best weapon
in the pads of her fingers
and in her mirror. She will be able
to detect immediately any abnormalities
as soon as they appear. Or at least
she should, working clockwise
around her breast, reclining
on a towel to spread the unruly breast.
Emphasis is placed on the danger area
the upper, outer quadrant,
but all of it, the breast, the armpit
are the war zone. She must be thorough

in her sensitive sweeps across the landscape
of her chest. The weapon is of no use
if it isn't used regularly. Even so,
there is no guarantee. The enemy
often sneaks across the border,
lays claim to territory, digs in.
Skilled medical minds
stand ready to raze
where the danger lurks and beyond.
Collateral damage is often necessary.

Become a Nest
Maryann Russo, Palos Verdes Estates, CA

A place woven
with forsaken things,
brittle twigs, dry leaves,
mud of dung and dirt,
shards of broken hearts,
shattered shells and
slivers of hope
built on a branch,
nestled in the brush
for no one to find.

Become a nest
for all that is unforgiven,
the hidden hates,
the disdain of what pride
could not conquer,
a nest for all
that is lost and
never found,
each single earring
and crumpled bill,
every dream forgotten
in a slump of restless sleep.

Become that nest,
open and ready
to hold whatever
longs to be born,
longs to be let go,
longs to be wingèd.

Résumé
Ura Shi, Palo Alto, CA

A list of clubs   little things i do for fun

Leadership positions   little things

      Opportunities   i

a list full of nothing — nothing i care   do

for   for

things I don't have time for   fun

burdens   —for fun?

                     right, that was the question

It'll pay off

      —are you sure?   out of each and every one i've

striving for a dream dreamt   answered

half-awake   *full score, too*

     is it real?

a fire ignited once again   this one's so much harder

on barely-there fuel

               too busy

—I can do this   to-do lists

Won't it be fun?   *—filled*

               mind

i need to do this   *—filled*

won't it look good on that résumé?   calendar

               —filled

application questions   inbox

               —filled

What are your hobbies? eyes

—what are my hobbies?   empty

Solstice
Monica Mills, Maplewood, NJ

That dark-eyed spirit left pink Post-its on my door:
maintenance was here/ nothing was stolen
Smeared letters scribbled on a line.
The penmanship wasn't mine, no answer
upon knocking. I steadied my breath,
strode through that threshold alone, found
someone else's home in earnest discomfort.

A labyrinthine landscape of Eden. Deific mountains
crowned themselves in ice. Frost-bitten rain fell flinching
to the earth. Each teardrop's mournful sting slowly
staggering from heaven like water unsure which state
its penance should take. Daylight's blinding brightness
made no atonement for the slush. Cruel, white,
and all else empty as the mortal eye could see.

A song, furtive and soft, soon found my frost-numbed ears
like the rustle of pine-needles kissing northern wind,
apparitions swept into the day. Lost shades splintered
in sleet-wrecked sun. Their lingering eyes berating
my opaque body like beings of tempered glass refracting
the light that mirrors will touch but won't marry.

Scent of smog-packed snow hung low, burned
the back of my throat like smoke of newborn brushfires
on ancient, craggy, summits. I turned to go, my shadow
born unto trouble, my caste not welcome in such glacial
places, but the passage I'd taken had shut. No trail blazes
on display. Dear, winter has come to stay its silver hour.
When all else fades you'll find a key beneath the mat.
Steal what you please. I'm not coming back.

Redwood Souls
Lauren Jeffers, Menlo Park, CA

My steps are soft in the Redwoods
Eyes: Watching
trailing the paths of sun-spun gold,
that cling to the trees like spider silk.
Light bleeding through the treetops,
staining wisened moss in hues of skylit tears
brushing my skin in warmth.
—redwoods—
Glowing as Apollo spools across the woods,
—as ink in water—
the sun god drifts across the forest floor—
burning up star-kissed shadows,
dappling creeping vines.
—crimson—
my body: Still
still as ancient mountains
still as starlit skies
—still—
as if the redwoods could swallow me whole.
Staring as the clouds thicken
Apollo cowers and Icarus falls
—the sun—
gone.
the world falls into the darkness of a universe forgotten
and I: Alone

The Hedonists
Katie Cavicchio, Latrobe PA

Do you remember how we ate
in our first house? Standing
in the garden biting into ripe tomatoes,
cracking our chickens' eggs into hot pans,
making pesto because one of us
brought home fresh pasta.

Do you remember how impulsive we were?
Like each meal was a feast, like
we knew those animal days were
a moment in time, not made to last
but made to look
back on as the routines of middle-age took shape,
Now, calling for a pizza on a Friday night
a wild act – *yeah, we can still party* –

but if it's possible, I love you more today.
Watching you reach for the family-size
box of cereal with marshmallows and
hand it to our daughter in the cart, I see
you as you were, sinew and muscle
and hair streaked blond, holding
up a jalapeno, talking about salsa.

The Polaroid I Bought
Calloway Song, Taipei, Taiwan

& used once. The picture was taken
in some fog you could tap the shoulder of:

it was arriving five minutes too
late & too far, as always. Like

looking through that telescope I
bought after hearing the shimmering

penny dancing between my fingers
can be some novelty we don't have
a name for, yet, waves like sound

change as they approach & drift afar

& became the *Doppler effect*—I thought
of a friend, but forgot where he went.

I wonder if he's still driving the same
Mercedes his parents bought before

marriage. Said they divorced but his dad
still wears the ring & hides it like a scar. I

needed my glasses to see far so I took
them off. The pollen in the air was naïve like

me, believing life could grow from
the smallest cervices. I wanted to chase

a speck like a bubble, hold it like
a friend I always had, whose name

I lost. I sat back down & brushed off
the seat next to me waiting—

Bloodline
Sasha Ovalle, Los Angeles, CA

Gold, bright as it may gleam, no longer holds its past allure.
Nor does the twinkling gem that sits upon the ring so pure,
Treasures that once gave rise to endless war and strife,
All dethroned by the most primal of fluids, the essence of life.

Taught to cast it scornfully at frauds and schemers,
Now the masses kneel before it as the ultimate redeemer.
For that liquid, shared in our slovenly kiss,
Is the stuff of dreams, a portal to untold bliss.

To be me, or not to be me? The longing for the latter is profound,
As science unravels the secrets of my DNA, its guts unwound.
With genetic sight they carefully separate strands from soul.
Oh, hail the prophets, who fill the infinite hole!

The transparency of our desires, stark against the night.
Foolish as the helpless host who covets the power of the parasite.
Banish those fears, for your story is yet to be told,
Perhaps a descendant of kings, or a baron of old.

From the tyranny of bloodline, we once fought to break free,
Only to cling to its leg with feral ferocity.
We forget there's a fate worse than failure, in idleness it lies,
But the shine of procrastination often catches our eyes.

As a child of humble roots, I join the salivary quest,
To unlock hidden secrets in my family crest.
Alas, the palmist opens the mysterious door,
Revealing that I am exactly who I was before.

In All My Seriousness
Ilaria, New South Wales, Australia

Of course, you didn't know,

I mean, how could you?

I have always been told

that I would make a superb actress.

For I lied to you,

when I said

I didn't want anything serious.

If you actually knew me,

you would have known

that I have always been a serious person

and that I wanted you,

in all my seriousness.

What Am I Waiting For?
Katherine Johnson, Denver, CO

One hour set aside
Clear and tidy desk top
Select the paper, sharpen pencils
Fire up computer

Almost forgot – brush teeth
Make that dentist appointment
Adjust the paper
Find my favorite pen

A bit chilly
Get a sweater
Add a colorful scarf
Tie it just right

Back at the desk
Journal or start an essay
Reread my last attempt
Not very good, needs work

Make a cup of tea
Boil the water
Swish the tea bag
Add a bit of honey

Ah– that's better
15 min left
What am I waiting for
Inspiration

The perfect topic
The perfect phrase
The perfect word
Just write

Doorbell rings
Open package
Time's up
Maybe tomorrow…

I think Jesus and I are on good terms
Amanda Garcia, Austin, TX

I think jesus and I are on good terms
      I stayed awake too late last night watching
            neon bodies dance on my screen
The Lord bless you and keep you;
          I thought about your lips in church today
      the flowers you gave me last week are wilting
the Lord make his face shine upon you
         I wonder if my lipstick is too red
             You left a strand of hair on my pillow
        The priest says we are okay
     and be gracious to you;
there are ashes on my forehead
         i think jesus and I are on good terms
      take my body, eat it whole
the Lord turn his face toward you
               Your lipstick stains on my wine glass
          This is my blood, I shed it for you
           I am on my knees on a Sunday morning
        I think my flowers just need a new vase
         Do you think Jesus and i are on good terms
I wonder if my dress is too short
              kneel, i said
The table is for everybody
              kneel, i said
                Kneel
    I'm pressing my hands together
Lord, hear me cry
      As long as it is behind closed doors
    and give you peace.
         Do you think I'll get into heaven?

A Father's Day Poem
Ayana Monet, Los Angeles, CA

biased daughter

entrusted to glean from her fraction of time

during his 70 plus years

Caribbean father to make proud

disciplinarian with oratory prowess and quiet lion command

the pancake maker

risen from humble places

Calypsonian fame begat Berklee dreams

adventurous spirit projected futuristic

joining the tech boom in the nick of time

unpredictable

beginnings

1945

born from two souls

later orphaned but not alone

family survived

dared to thrive

Trinidadian trumpeting red, black and white pride

then American red, white and blue

fell for a woman of Jamaican black, green and gold

kept a humble heart

wrapped in love, sacrifice and steady beats

struggles turned opportunity

for the next of kin to take command of their own futuristic music

Before the Bell Rings
Will Arndt, Salem, MA

First day of faculty meetings
before the new year.
First session:
"Active Shooter Response Training"

"What is normal?"
asks the beefy consultant,
encouraging us to look around
notice our surroundings.
"Be present"
Not mindful,
but vigilant
to assess potential threats.

We then watch
a video on how and when to apply
tourniquets, a PSA called
"Stop the Bleed."

"It doesn't have to be this way!"
the narrator cheerily reminds us.

Next we practice building
barricades, our first ice breaker of the year.
And after we learn
to "swarm," to work together
to mob and immobilize an assailant

having been taught the parts and pieces
of a rifle in order
to safely wrench a weapon away.

"Flip the script
on shooters!" the ex-cop encourages.

As if the next episode
were inevitable—
       the roles already cast,
       the cameras ready,
       and everyone knows their lines.

We're ready

for thoughts and prayers.

This Poem Is Not About You
Lexie DeRiggi, Allison Park, PA

I swear as I consider the ways in which
a body befriends friction.
You and I behave like motion
until inertia's been all but spent and
I'm left searching for something
more essential, central.
I want my nerves left raw as a brand new wound,
the sink of teeth, a thumb-pressed bruise,
the blade wrenched out.
And phonetic sounds
simply don't satisfy
when I crave that old complexity—
and if this is a simple question of merit,
maybe I just haven't earned my momentary stay.
Crashing confusion,
some of yours, some of mine,
throbs in the liminals.
Tell me I'm not for nothing.
Rip me from the middle distance.
This poem is about me.
This poem is not about you.
Do I sound convincing yet?

Orion
Lukas English, Austin, TX

Sometimes I am asked about my sign.
"Aquarius," I'll say –
born beneath the ebb and flow
of the February night sky.
I don't believe
in astrological ideas and coincidences,
but eighteen years ago last week,
the Sun kissed my back seven times.
One, two: shoulders.
Strong enough to bear the weight
of all that the world could throw.
Three, four, five: a belt.
Tight enough to hold me close
across wretched seas and bumpy roads.
Six, seven: legs.
Ambitious enough to push me
to astronomical heights.
Our yellow giant,
giver of light, life, and burns,
begot seven brown dwarfs
to freckle my pale universe –
chosen to be a cosmic crusader.

All God's Children in the New Orleans Airport
Mary Brandt, Houston, TX

The ten year old in a white tutu
purple tights
awesome high tops
and a T-shirt that said

Be brave
Be brave
Be brave
Be brave

The five year old in the restroom who announced
(to everyone)
"Be sure to wash your hands"

The young black men with sculpted hair
The Asian guy with pink pants and a sway

Those who hold hands (or not)
In wheelchairs (or not)
With beards in a braid

Sheriffs on Segways
The people sitting at the bar

All who carry backpacks.

Be brave
Be brave
Be brave
Be brave

Made in the USA
Coppell, TX
15 December 2023